HAUS CURIOSITIES

*Justice in Public Life*

# About the Contributors

**Claire Foster-Gilbert** is the Founder Director of Westminster Abbey Institute. A public philosopher and author, Foster-Gilbert has played an instrumental role in the fields of medical research ethics and environmental issues.

**James Hawkey** is Canon Theologian of Westminster Abbey and Chair of Westminster Abbey Institute. Hawkey is a Bye-Fellow of Clare College, Cambridge, visiting Lecturer at King's College London, and Chaplain to HM The Queen.

**Jane Sinclair** was Canon Rector of St Margaret's Church, Westminster Abbey and Chair of Westminster Abbey Institute. Earlier, she was Archdeacon of Stow and Lindsey in the Diocese of Lincoln, and worked in parish and cathedral ministry and in theological education.

On 14 January 2021, Jane died of cancer. In death as in life, she faced the joy and tragedy of the human condition with clear-sighted compassion and courage, reflected in her essay, which we are honoured to include in this volume.

Edited and with an introduction by
Claire Foster-Gilbert

## JUSTICE IN PUBLIC LIFE

Claire Foster-Gilbert, James Hawkey and Jane Sinclair

First published by Haus Publishing in 2021
4 Cinnamon Row
London SW11 3TW
*www.hauspublishing.com*

A CIP catalogue record for this book is
available from the British Library

Print ISBN: 978-1-913368-20-3
Ebook ISBN: 978-1-913368-21-0

Typeset in Garamond by MacGuru Ltd

Printed in Czech Republic

# Contents

In memoriam Jane Sinclair 1956–2021

# Acknowledgements

Sincere thanks are due to the Dean and Chapter of Westminster, the Council of Reference and Steering Group of Westminster Abbey Institute, Asha Astley, Edoardo Braschi, Elizabeth Butler-Sloss, Gillian Cooper, Harry Hall, Alice Horne, Aneta Horniak, Kathleen James, Eleanor Lovegrove, Seán Moore, Mark Ormerod, Barbara Schwepcke, Jo Stimfield, and Jack Straw.

# Introduction

*Claire Foster-Gilbert*

Justice is a virtue to be desired in public life every bit as much as truth. And like truth, it has never been seen in its fullness. There is no perfectly just person, perfectly just institution, or perfectly just society. And yet we can only know this to be true because we have a sense of what it means to be unjust and, as a result, just – even if we have never seen it in its perfection. Moreover, we want it: not only to be treated justly but also to be just ourselves and to work within just institutions. We want our societies to be just, and that requires both our public servants and the institutions through which they work to be just: Parliament, government, judiciary, schools and universities, the health service, the police and armed forces, and so on.

The visiting of justice upon the public has to be willingly received, as responses to the COVID-19 pandemic have shown: think of the many businesses who have supported national lockdowns despite the devastating impact on their finances. If we trust our public service institutions, we are likely to accept just decisions even if they are not directly in our interests. If we don't trust them, we might take justice into our own hands, for example by spurning the offer of a vaccine against COVID-19, or, in other, more extreme circumstances setting up vigilante groups for self-protection. Justice holds the peace; without it, we hold each other at arm's length with whatever means we have. Justice makes it possible to view the other as neighbour, not potential enemy.

The essays in this book, which delve into the issue of justice, are edited versions of lectures delivered in Westminster Abbey in 2019, intended primarily for audiences of public servants and all those interested in the role of justice within public service. The essays explore, respectively, what justice is; institutional justice; and justice in society. Each essay makes the case for working towards justice, even though it is always a work in progress, always a journey, never an arrival. The essays approach the subject in very different ways, but they all concur on two things: that justice has to be embodied, enacted, brought to life in each of us, and yet it can only be achieved in relationships, not by individuals.

In 'Fair Enough? A Vision for Justice in the Twenty-first Century', James Hawkey offers a scholarly and comprehensive exploration of the nature of justice.

His findings make evident that 'fairness' is far too thin a concept for the purposes of justice; we do not mean, when we seek to do each other justice, that we simply give each other what (we think) is deserved. Who are we, that justice should be offered? Understanding justice requires an account of human identity. Further exploration reveals that justice is inescapably wedded to truth, and it is always relational. Hawkey thus offers a refreshing and reinvigorated means to navigate towards justice through the complexities of the twenty-first century: by means of truth-seeking and truth-telling, and always in a community context. He then provides examples of these navigational tools in use in Leeds, New Zealand, and Finland, and in the practical application of restorative justice.

My essay 'Can Institutions Be Just?' seeks to plumb the depths of the apparent disparity between just individuals and the often dehumanising effects of institutions, even those created explicitly to serve justice. Why is it that institutions seem to leach the energy of individual responses to injustice? But can justice survive without institutions to mete it out? How far can individual enthusiasm take us? I argue that we cannot do without institutions, difficult though they can make our lives, and that it is right to use our time and energy to work to ensure that institutions themselves remain just.

This is especially true of the ancient, slow-growing institutions of public service. My essay identifies three threats to institutional justice: where the institution employs unjust acts to achieve the goals for which it was created, using the desirability of the goal as an excuse, a danger especially present in 'virtuous' institutions whose aim is to serve the public; where those working in an institution find themselves serving the institution instead of the purpose of the institution; and when the institution becomes corroded and even corrupted, perpetuating unjust behaviour. In each case, the threats are subject to human agency, both in their existence and in their prevention. At the end of the essay, I retain some of the questions and answers from the original lecture, as they expand the points made.

Jane Sinclair asks, 'Is a Just Society Possible?' She writes compellingly of Rotherham, where she was vicar when shocking acts of abuse against young white women were perpetrated by British-Pakistani men. Sinclair does not flinch from telling the truth of this story, and she goes on to tell with equal clarity the truth about poverty and inequality today. Her account is supported by what has come to light through the COVID-19 pandemic. From this honest and distressing start, Sinclair proposes what it is that gives rise to such societal injustices: human nature in its Hobbesian form; our inheritance of unjust social structures and skewed expectations; the wide range of views over what constitutes justice and just behaviour; and the difficulty of ensuring just behaviour between nation states. Sinclair does not dismiss these challenges but rather explores them fully. Her conclusions about the possibility of justice in society are nevertheless hopeful; she makes a plea to our better selves.

Each essay, then, remorselessly reminds the reader of their own agency, of their personal moral responsibility to navigate their way towards justice. And each essay confirms that the journey is still always made with others. Justice in public life is crucial; its existence depends on all of us.

# Fair Enough? A Vision for Justice in the Twenty-First Century

*James Hawkey*

'Fair enough' is a laconic, chiefly British phrase people use when they are reluctant to admit that they disagree with each other. But, as I shall argue in this essay, 'fairness' is never actually quite enough in situations which demand justice. I begin with two straightforward points: first, justice is always threatened when truth is a casualty. No outcome or agreement can be truly just when truth has been squandered, ignored, or placed anywhere other than at the heart of the conversation. Second, contemporary public discourse – notably but not solely in so-called 'justice issues' – often seems to confuse fairness, and its associated emotions, with justice *per se*. Culturally, we need to become more conscious of these themes of truth and justice at a time when slogans can replace principled argument, and as repeated assertions drown out careful analysis of complex data or evidence. A 'thin' notion of fairness simply does not take the deep truth of questions related to the human person seriously enough.

This is not an essay on criminal justice; rather, it explores more general principles. However, it is important to note that criminal justice does not exist in a separate category, unrelated to other expressions of justice. Criminal justice should serve the common good in a particular way. Exploring how legality and justice depend on each other, Nigel Simmonds argues, 'the institution of law as such can be rendered intelligible only when we discern its relationship to certain moral values'.[1] He discusses how the pursuit of the law and the passing of judgment are dependent on a shared 'inherited vocabulary of moral ideas'.[2] In other words, justice, truth, and law, for example, should be in permanent and creative relationship with one another. I explore this kind of relationship first, before discussing various examples of how a focus on justice as a virtue rooted in truth-seeking and truth-telling might help us navigate the complexities of the twenty-first century as related to economic justice, eco-justice, social justice, and restorative justice. The COVID-19 pandemic has highlighted an additional point of relevance: in a world traumatised by sickness, uncertainty, and economic collapse, secular democracies will become increasingly vulnerable unless they have more explicit awareness that justice is also an expression of solidarity.

## A voice from the mountain

In his famous speech delivered in Memphis the night before his assassination in April 1968, Martin Luther King Jr uses Jesus's parable of the Good Samaritan (Luke 10: 30–37) to outline his own struggle as being principally one of justice, the outworking of which he calls 'dangerous unselfishness'.[3] The Good Samaritan story is about neighbourliness and difference, and it plays out in the lives of figures associated with the respectable religious establishment – the priest and the Levite – and a foreign outcast, the Samaritan. You may remember the tale: a lawyer asks Jesus, 'Who is my neighbour?', and Jesus responds by recounting how a traveller on the road from Jerusalem to Jericho was robbed, beaten, and left to die. Two members of the religious establishment, a priest and a Levite, pass him by, probably conscious of their own need for ritual purity and their safety. It is a Samaritan (an outcast) who takes pity on the man and cares for him. Within their own normative structures, it's quite possible to argue that both priest and Levite acted *fairly*, in terms of their own tribes' expectations. But it is the Samaritan who shows us what justice looks like. As well as offering immediate help, the Samaritan commits to long-term care, escorts the beaten man to an inn, underwrites the cost of ongoing treatment, and ensures that this nameless stranger is restored to full health.

King recounts from his own experience of driving it that the Jericho Road is a particularly treacherous one: there were all sorts of reasons why otherwise good people might not have wanted to stop. But the fundamental difference between the Samaritan and the others is that instead of asking what might happen to *him* if he stopped, at the forefront of his mind was what would transpire for *the beaten man* if he did not stop. The Samaritan engages, acts justly and kindly towards the man, and reveals that the circles of neighbours and outcasts – friends and enemies – overlap.

In King's speech, he ponders whether priest and Levite might have been on their way to a meeting of the Jericho Road Improvement Association: 'Maybe they felt that it was better to deal with the problem from the causal root, rather than to get bogged down with an individual effect.' We've all known plenty of such committees, their good intentions, and occasional good results. But the point is, justice compelled the Samaritan to stop. In all the wide and varied theological, juridical, sociological, and philosophical commentary on this parable over the last 2,000 years, at its heart is a person-centred vision of justice that can be owned and operated by a community. In practice, this is quite a challenge. Which societies, groups, cultures, have ever really managed to work this out with integrity? It is at least as much of a challenge for our time as for any other. But in a society which is increasingly fragmented and divided, it is perhaps increasingly urgent to lay down this particular gauntlet once again. It might have been considered 'fair enough' for both Levite and priest to pass by on the other side of a dangerous and exposed road, but it certainly wasn't just. Justice is primarily a relational dynamic.[4]

## The *imago Dei*

Before going any further, perhaps we need to ask what makes the human person worth attending to at all. Famously, Aristotle, who is at the root of what we think of as the 'virtue' tradition, taught that justice meant giving people what they deserve. But why might people deserve justice, and why – particularly, but perhaps not solely, in matters relating to human beings – is establishing some supposedly neutral benchmark of 'fairness' not sufficient?

Judaeo-Christian belief points us towards the concept of the *imago Dei*: the belief that each human being is made in the image and likeness of God, with the divine law inscribed in the human heart. The inner gift of conscience and the observable natural law provide a clear template for virtuous living and allow human beings to play a rational and moral role in social and political life. However, this bottom line is problematic for people who don't espouse a religious world view, as well as for those who conclude that particular religious beliefs should not hold traction within the public arena because they are not seen to convene sufficiently broad support.[5] It may be that, as the world once again becomes increasingly religious, this central tenet of Jewish and Christian teaching will re-enter the public and political consciousness.[6] In the meantime, perhaps there is practical common sense in John Rawls's argument that foundational concepts for the creation of laws and communities must rest on 'plain truths now widely accepted, and available, to citizens generally'.[7] We will engage a little more with Rawls later on, but if the notion of the *imago Dei* really is not one that can be owned within and between cultures, where else might we look for a solid foundation for a further discussion of justice?

## Human rights

The Universal Declaration of Human Rights, proclaimed by the United Nations General Assembly in December 1948, has been translated into over 500 languages.[8] Without understating the UN's considerable problems and challenges, this accomplishment stands as one of the most important benchmarks of modern times, and it is well worth revisiting at moments of crisis and tension.

The declaration's preamble recognises the 'inherent

dignity and ... equal and inalienable rights of all members of the human family' as 'the foundation of freedom, justice and peace in the world'. Although an initial proposal to include a reference to humanity's creation in the image of God was rejected for fear that it could limit its appeal, one might argue that the declaration proposes precisely this. Dignity instead of sanctity; 'sanctity of life' under a different name, if you like. Two years earlier, a preamble to the UN founding charter had been drafted by the former South African Prime Minister Jan Smuts, in which he insisted on the 'dignity and worth' of the human person. Smuts also proposed an additional first chapter enshrining four specific beliefs, among them 'faith in human rights, the sacredness, essential worth and integrity of the human personality'. The preamble was accepted, although the rather more explicitly religious language about the *sanctity* of human life in a new first chapter was not.[9] However, the 'inherent *dignity*' mentioned in the Declaration of Human Rights implicitly insists on mutual accountability as a central moral and social reality to which justice must relate. It is this inherent dignity, for example, that allows us to call apartheid evil and that obliges us to work to end the injustice of human trafficking.

But no matter how compelling the discourse of human rights, we should be aware, at least in practice, of two competing approaches, which have led the philosopher Bruce Williams to call for a 'bilingual dialogue'[10] between them. The 'subjective' approach, found in the declaration, begins with the human person as the subject, so rights are understood as claims that the individual or subject is morally empowered to make. An 'objective' approach, meanwhile, begins with society or community and sees rights as necessary for maintaining or restoring balance between the elements of the social whole in order to secure the common good.

The latter approach is at the fore of the classical and medieval traditions. While St Thomas Aquinas, for example, has much to say about the unique dignity of each human person created in the *imago Dei*, he does not have a theory of human rights in our modern sense. When Aquinas speaks of right or *ius* as the object of justice, he is not thinking about satisfying a particular individual's claim to something; rather, he speaks of that which is just, that which is *objectively* due in a given interaction within a community. Both approaches – the subjective and the objective – have particular strengths. Think of the inherent rights of an individual which, when they are threatened by a mob, are protected by a subjective approach. On the other hand, an objective approach pursues the common good and seeks social harmony. Both these approaches have strong roots in the virtue of justice, which we must now examine explicitly.

## Justice itself

Gallons of ink have been spilt on the question of justice, from Aristotle to Augustine, Aquinas, Kant, Macintyre, and Rawls. These great thinkers are naturally figures of their own time, but each has contributed specific insights that resonate across the centuries. The *Summa Theologiae* of St Thomas Aquinas is a remarkable achievement of philosophy and theology. It shaped medieval and late medieval culture probably more than any other nonscriptural book. Reliant on Aristotle and Augustine, as well as integrating insights from the Islamic tradition which may well otherwise have been lost, Thomas pursues the question of justice as a cardinal virtue. 'Cardinal' comes from the Latin *cardo* (heart), indicating that, alongside temperance, prudence, and courage, justice is a basic requirement for a moral life. For Thomas, such a life is rooted in the given, knowable, and observable natural law. Fundamentally, all goodness, all justice, finds its origin in that supreme good we call God.[11]

In the *Summa*, Thomas investigates justice as a question of personal behaviour, or rendering someone 'their due'. In other words, the act of justice is 'rendering to everyone what is [rightfully] theirs'.[12] The virtues are learned by practice, which is to say that justice should shape the *habit* of giving others their due, so that ultimately we are firmly committed to doing so at all times. This is key. It is possible to give others their due even without the virtue of justice, for example when the 'other' happens to be someone for whom we have a special affection, or when giving another their due serves our own advantage. However – and here comes the rub – when this involves some inconvenience to ourselves, or if we have no special concern for the other person, we may not be so readily inclined to render what is due. We thus need the virtue of justice to incline us consistently toward giving others their due, whether or not we find it advantageous or rewarding to do so. This habit builds just communities, groups, families, and nations.

Thomas proceeds to discuss various kinds of justice, both general (for the good of the community) and particular (focused on certain people or groups of people). The common good, he argues, is the overarching principle that ultimately governs all justice, including legal justice. After considering many detailed sub-questions, Thomas moves on to discuss other virtues necessarily allied to justice. Two that are particularly important to this discussion are the virtues of truth and equity. Truthfulness denotes the virtue disposing us to speak and act in ways that are consistent with our inner thoughts, at an appropriate time and in an appropriate manner.[13] Following Aristotle, Thomas insists that equity (*epieikeia*, or reasonableness) is also allied to justice. Moreover, he deems equity the preeminent realisation of justice, surpassing and regulating even legal justice itself,[14] writing of moments when the letter of the law should be 'set aside' to 'follow the dictates of justice and the common good'.[15] Legal frameworks simply cannot take into account every possible contingency that would warrant an exception in the application of the law, so equity is needed to ensure justice; this essential malleability and dynamism is essential to justice itself, even if it can be exploited by proponents of situation ethics.

The late twentieth century saw a renewal of interest in this broadly Aristotelian/Thomist world view. Importantly, this has not solely been the preserve of self-consciously religious people.[16] Two further developments have refreshed a 'virtue' agenda at the heart of how many Christians now intuitively think about justice. First, the reception of Catholic Social Teaching as a gift for the wider human community as it relates to wide-ranging issues of human dignity from migration to prisons policy, and, since the Second Vatican Council in the 1960s, the Catholic Church's own explicit support of the principles of human rights. To quote the *Compendium of the Social Doctrine of the Church*: 'The Church

sees in these [human] rights the extraordinary opportunity that our modern times offer, through the affir-
mation of these rights, for more effectively recognising
human dignity and universally promoting it as a characteristic inscribed by God the Creator in his creature.'[17]

A commitment to the universal applicability of human
rights fused with an insistence on virtue has created what
is, for many, an attractive system. Back in 1999, Pope St
John Paul II, when addressing a multifaith audience
on the World Day of Peace, insisted that 'no one can
legitimately deprive another person, whoever they may
be, of these rights, since this would do violence to their
nature'.[18] This fusion of human rights language with principles drawn from the heart of the virtue tradition has
helped much Christian teaching on the human person to
be received more broadly. It has also arguably contributed
to the Catholic Church's self-confidence in finally declar-
ing the death penalty inadmissible in August 2018.[19]

In England, an impressive number of Anglican writers
have contributed to the conversation.[20] Two of Angli-
canism's most distinguished and influential voices on
this topic are R. H. Tawney and William Temple, both
influenced by British Idealism[21] and believing in the
social nature of human beings, as well as in an 'Absolute'
discernible by reason. As they articulated their visions of
a more just society, neither found the category 'equality'

strong enough.[22] Temple spoke of it in carefully couched terms. Recalling that equality was ruthlessly applied in Maximilien Robespierre's France to devastating effect, Temple falls back on language that sits comfortably within a human rights framework, praising 'equality of inherent worth and of the right of every individual to be himself'.[23] This argument proceeds from the fundamental truth about human beings themselves and, as such, is rooted close to Aristotle and Thomas.

Of all the political philosophers currently working in this tradition, the Harvard professor Michael J. Sandel is perhaps the best known. In his book *Justice: What's the Right Thing to Do?*, Sandel poses the question of whether the state should – or could – judge what is virtue and what is vice. Can there be an agreed framework in the twenty-first century where such a project would flourish? Sandel argues that such a framework is needed, and he uses the example of a deal sealed by contract to explain why. The simple fact of a contract existing, he argues, is not sufficient to make it fair – let alone just. To establish whether or not the contract is fair, some kind of independent standard is needed.[24]

Sandel is well known as a critic of the liberalism of writers such as John Rawls, whose sense of justice as fairness dismisses any metaphysical or normative notion of 'the good'.[25] In a famous thought experiment, Rawls invites us to imagine that we are all ignorant of our own and one another's real-world status, background, and behaviour. What principles would we choose as the basis of a new society in which we will live? Rawls maintains that this 'veil of ignorance' would free us of cognitive biases and lead us to produce an egalitarian society in which no group is disadvantaged. At first glance, this argument posits a certain hopefulness about the human spirit. But from what we know of the complexity of the human person, could we be confident that such a project would not be characterised by untrustworthiness, unpredictability, or chaos? Twentieth-century totalitarianism revealed all too clearly that majorities do not necessarily veer naturally towards the good. But there is a deeper social point at play here too: human beings cannot be detached from their culture, commitments, and characteristics, because these features make us who we are.[26] We cannot face the demands of justice without taking seriously 'the *real* demands of *real* societies that have *real* commitments to understandings of the good. There is no "view from nowhere"'.[27]

Those engaged in any kind of negotiation or mediation know that to gain traction with your opposite number, you must either find some degree of common ground or be able to empathise with your neighbour. The great problem for Rawls is that without a shared concept of the 'good', any contract or negotiation is at risk of leading to injustice or exploitation. Especially in serious matters of ethics and welfare, as Sandel puts it, we 'cannot remain neutral toward competing conceptions of the good life'.[28] Towards the end of his book, Sandel outlines three potential visions of justice: first, the utilitarian approach, which takes as its root the greatest happiness for the greatest number; second, in a free world and a free market, perhaps justice simply means respecting individual choice; the third approach conceives of justice as cultivating virtue and shaping the common good.[29] Broadly speaking, I suggest this last vision, in which individuals and communities encourage one another in seeking truth rather than relying on weaker indicators, is going to be necessary in the twenty-first century – as long as this is tempered with equity and rooted in a strong commitment to human rights.

I hope it will be clear by now that questions of justice are necessarily linked to questions of identity: who and what demands our respect? What can, and what can't, be treated as a non-moral disposable utility? In other words, who is my neighbour? We live at a time of considerable conceptual fluidity around questions of alliances, regions, and blocs, as well as how macro questions of politics and geography map themselves onto individual lives whose dignity demands our solidarity. The refugee crisis reveals this particularly sharply. In the context of overlapping cultures that are themselves changing faster than we can perceive – domestically as well as globally – we need to work for a shared commitment to justice, and therefore truth, without hiding behind the much easier language of 'values', which is itself too nebulous and potentially ideologically divisive. In this final section, I want to consider four situations in which we see an out-working of justice that is allied to truth and equity and that is rooted in a clear commitment to fundamental human rights. Each of these short examples exposes a foundational confidence in what society might be, and in what the human person really is.

**Leeds Poverty Truth Commission**

The Leeds Poverty Truth Commission was established in 2014 to enable politicians, journalists, leaders in industry and business, policy developers, and those in the third sector to work together alongside local people affected by the reality of poverty to help the city tackle both cause and effect. In other words, the commission worked to bring evidence into the room, as suggested by its slogan: 'Nothing without us, [that is] about us, can be for us.' Andrew Grinnell, who established the commission, recalls how, prior to this, public officials were unintentionally positioned against local people in meetings.

Theories were discussed and policies set by those with little first-hand knowledge of issues, while inequality seemed to get worse. Grinnell writes, 'despite [a lot of] time, energy and resources being put into reversing the trend, the gap between rich and poor was widening. If we were to narrow the gap, there needed to be a change in the way the city responded to poverty.'[30] Through a combination of research and careful preparation, the group of civic and business leaders alongside fifteen people with ongoing experience of poverty led to 'a celebration of dignity ... as the "voiceless discovered their voices"'.

Grinnell's point is simple: justice requires truth-telling, and many solutions that could be described as 'fair' can also be inherently unjust. He tells the story of one commissioner arriving at a meeting particularly distressed, having received two bills that morning totalling £2,000. When moving between jobs, she had been misadvised and, as a result, had not filled in the correct forms. She now had to repay money that she'd been overpaid. A local business commissioner said to her, 'I don't know how you carry on. You try to do the right thing, and from what you've told me, something always seems to go wrong.' The same day, another commissioner told of the challenges posed by national rules in how benefits might be distributed. He explained his conundrum, and the same individual who had arrived distressed said, 'I don't know how you do your job. You're a good bloke doing this for the right reasons. Except you can't always do the right thing because people who don't understand or seem to care about us are telling you how to do it.' In this case, justice would have been aided by greater trust in local analysis, local decision-making, and through involving in the conversation the very people the policies were directed towards. In other words, when it comes to applying justice in local situations, we should remember the principle of subsidiarity.

Poverty frequently dehumanises people and disconnects them. The commission's 'HuManifesto'[31] explains that social problems are best solved through building relationships. Right at the heart of this work is the diagnosis that injustice is an issue for the whole of society rather than a problem to be solved for or by individuals. In his encyclical *Fratelli tutti*, Pope Francis develops this concept by arguing for forms of social friendship: '[while] individuals can help others in need, when they join together in initiating social processes of fraternity and justice for all, they enter "the field of charity at its most vast, namely political charity"'.[32] The pope goes on to argue that social and political charity find their expression in 'macro-relationships: social, economic and political', and that this kind of social awareness 'makes us effectively seek the good of all people, considered not *only* as individuals or private persons, but also in the social dimension that unites them. Each of us is fully a person when we are part of a people; at the same time, there are no peoples without respect for the individuality of each person'.[33] In doing so, Pope Francis sets out a vision of what it is to truly be *members* of a society: individuals in networks of relationship that characterise what it is to be human, where individual rights and responsibility for one another go hand in hand.

## The New Zealand well-being budget

In 2019, the government of New Zealand committed itself to putting people's well-being and the environment at the heart of its budgetary policies, including reporting against a wider set of well-being indicators rather than simply relying on financial statistics.[34] Outlining the principles behind this ambitious plan, the government calls it a 'more rounded measure of success', 'supported by ... processes that facilitate evidence-based decisions'. The implicit assumption here is that the 'commercial' has in some senses eroded our social solidarity; that is to say that, when politics is captured by money on its own terms, social priorities are displaced, human dignity is no longer a priority, and it is harder to develop a sense of civic morality characterised by justice.

Two different commitments to truth are at play here.

First, we see the truth that the sanctity of human life and the dignity of the environment are to be served by financial policies and not subjugated to them. Second, in policy terms, this work is underpinned by serious research so that financial issues are determined in a context that focuses governmental priorities on real need. The five priorities currently outlined are: reducing child poverty; improving child well-being; addressing family violence; supporting mental well-being for all New Zealanders, with a special focus on those aged under twenty-four; and lifting Māori and Pacific Islander incomes, skills, and opportunities.

These priorities reveal a morality that focuses on the most vulnerable. They have their locus in the human rights/*imago Dei* traditions. Economic justice asks the question of who or what money serves. Money doesn't have a life of its own, as such; when money rules, or becomes a sole master, people and planet frequently suffer and the principles of justice are obscured. In *An Idol Unmasked*, Peter Selby asks, 'What kind of economy is it that submits us to an increase of quantitative thinking, volatility, and distraction?'[35] The simple answer, perhaps, is an unjust economy that treats human beings as commodities. The 2019 New Zealand budget, in contrast, represented a creative, virtue-led, and person-centred approach, which asks important questions about the sovereignty of money, and is focused on the *telos* or 'end goal' of human flourishing and fulfilment.

Furthermore, no discussion of justice in the twenty-first century should ignore the question of our natural environment. Climate change is increasingly a justice issue. The New Zealand proposals promise to create opportunities to transition to a sustainable and low-emission economy. If economic justice poses questions about the morality of markets and whether money serves the common good, eco-justice highlights questions about our relationship with the environment. One does not have to believe that creation is willed, good, or iconic to see that the relationship between the human person and the environment is a delicate ecosystem that is currently in crisis.

The French social scientist Bruno Latour goes further still. Claiming that we now live in 'the new Climatic Regime', his book *Down to Earth* outlines how climate change is right at the heart of 'all geopolitical issues' and that it is 'directly tied to questions of injustice'.[36] From the beginning of the book, Latour rails against cultural and political forces which have evacuated a sense of our common Earth through fantasy and irresponsibility; on the page usually reserved for dedications, the author somewhat provocatively quotes a senior member of the Trump administration: 'We've read enough books.'

Latour believes that the politics of truth-telling are crucial to the climate change issue, and he tears into a politics that he says has 'no object' because it rejects the world that it claims to inhabit. [37] Various issues are in Latour's sights here, not least globalisation and populism – both of which he claims are intrinsically unjust and fed by an unjust lack of truth-telling – but at heart he directs our attention back towards the Earth itself, given that for 200 years we have forgotten to 'anticipate the reactions of the terraqueous globe to human actions'.[38] Terms such as 'nature' are too vague for Latour; it is the very *Earth* that demands justice, with truth and equity.[39] As we begin the third millennium, how we respond to the health of our common home is a matter of justice, truth, and survival.

## Homelessness

My third example also comes from overseas, namely from Finland. Homelessness is a scourge throughout Europe – apart from in Finland, where it dropped by 35 per cent in the years 2010–2019.[40] Indeed, Finland is the only European country where homelessness continued to fall during the COVID-19 pandemic. Juha Kaakinen from the Housing First programme, which has had projects in the UK since 2016, explains how the Finnish approach 'takes housing as a basic human right' rather than it being conditional on homeless people engaging in treatment for addiction or mental health.[41] Insisting that the person is the subject of the policy alters conventional homelessness perspectives. An international review commissioned by the Finnish government[42] reveals the detailed complexity and strategic planning behind such a project. However, the results of the project speak for themselves: recovery rates from addiction are up, crime is down, and human beings do not have to attempt seemingly impossible self-rehabilitation in the 'chaos of the streets'.[43] Costs of social care and public health are falling as a result.

It would clearly be wrong to suggest that homelessness is a straightforward issue, or indeed to suggest that this is the only approach to the problem that could be characterised as *just*. It would be quite plausible to argue from criteria around public spending priorities, governmental time, and so on, that the Finnish approach is perhaps not quite *fair*. But if one believes that the good practice of justice tells the truth about the fundamental dignity of the human person, this approach is certainly both just and equitable. It is also one which expresses the kind of solidarity so desperately needed to ensure the health of a society.

## Restorative justice: telling the (ultimate) truth

My final example is a brief foray into criminal justice to consider practices that intensify the vision of justice I've been sketching. There are many reasons why restorative justice, which seeks to bring perpetrators and victims together, is to be widely encouraged, especially but not solely for first-time offenders. During 2018, restorative justice led to a 14 per cent reduction in reoffending across the UK.[44] Our prisons are currently overflowing, and the financial burden of custodial sentences is vast. Incarceration could therefore be reserved for those who pose a physical danger to society; some form of community service, combined with education, and coming face to face with the crime that has been committed, allows the social contract to be renewed in a just manner. Crime, after all, is violence against both justice and charity.

Restorative justice has ancient roots, even if a retributive system (that is, a system based on the theory of punishment) has been dominant throughout most of the last millennium in the West, and restorative means are still perceived as novel in some parts of criminal law.[45] The 1995 Truth and Reconciliation Commission in South Africa was an intense form of restorative justice which contributed to the building of a new society. Archbishop Desmond Tutu has written about how a series of Nuremberg-style trials for the perpetrators of apartheid abuse was neither viable nor desirable. He quotes the then Chief Justice of South Africa, Ismail Mahomed, discussing the process of a carefully negotiated transition: 'If the [new] constitution kept alive the prospect of continuous retaliation and revenge, the agreement of those threatened by its implementation might never have been forthcoming.'[46] The voting booth itself became a kind of purifying sanctuary.[47] Later, drawing on his own experience, Tutu was asked to advise the president of Rwanda in the aftermath of horrific genocide in that country. He writes, 'I told them that the cycle of reprisal and counter-reprisal that had characterised their national history had to be broken, and that the only way to do this was to go beyond retributive justice to restorative justice; to move on to forgiveness, because without it there was no future.'[48]

These principles can be applied locally. In practices of restorative justice, when criminals meet victims face to face, something much deeper than 'getting even' is going on: it restores not just particular relationships but the social fabric. For the Judaeo-Christian tradition, this also hints at the restoration of the whole of creation and a recognition of the intrinsic dignity of the human person, unconditional on how they have behaved. We have to consider the *telos* of our justice system in the twenty-first century. Is there a goal beyond getting even, beyond the supposed fairness that catches the headlines? Or are we content solely with the preservation of a status quo? Can we allow equity its own role in searching for the deep truth behind criminal action and its resolution? Practices of restorative justice help us build communities in which justice and its effects can be known and celebrated wholeheartedly.

## Conclusion

The Sala dei Nove of the Palazzo Pubblico in Siena, where the city state's magistracy would meet, was frescoed by Ambrogio Lorenzetti in 1338. Lorenzetti's cycle, *The Allegory of Good and Bad Government*, famously depicts the effects of good governance while offering stern warnings of what happens to both city and countryside when governance is bad. The principal picture sits above the doors through which the council entered the chamber, almost as if they emerged from Lorenzetti's allegorical realm itself.

The fresco is a masterpiece laden with meaning and symbolism. The figure of Justice is the only personified virtue to appear twice in the one picture, bookending the entire scene, as if the viewer is encouraged to read the whole picture again and again.[49] There is narrative in this image, but it is not strictly linear. It has to be observed and learned time after time: justice in the context of the other virtues and at the service of the Common Good, who is depicted off-centre and enthroned, looking rather like a Byzantine monarch. It seems probable that the Book of the Wisdom of Solomon – the first verse of which surrounds the head of the figure of Justice, divided in the same proportions as Dante's *Paradiso* – is the hermeneutical key to this painting.[50] The text 'Love justice [or righteousness], you rulers of the Earth' frames Justice and her scales like an extended halo, and the figure herself gazes up plaintively to an image of Wisdom, dropping a cord through her fingers to a depiction of Concordia, the personification of harmony, who in turn passes the thread on to the goodly citizens of the Republic of Siena. On one level, this is simply a profoundly beautiful piece of allegorical art, didactic in intent, reliant on Aristotle, and celebrating the age of Dante, who had died just over a decade earlier. As Hisham Matar puts it, 'If civic rule were a church, this would be its altarpiece.'[51]

But what makes this picture so extraordinary is its dynamism. We're used to figures of Justice holding scales or swords (as they do in Lorenzetti's fresco), but for there to be two figures holding one scene together, directing the Sienese citizenry on a journey of perpetual motion through the virtues, above the space where the council will sit in judgement, is a remarkable invitation to participate in an ongoing cycle of learning about justice – its practices, its implications, and its potential.

I have proposed that it is impossible to speak of justice without those allied virtues of truth and equity. Central to this thesis is a strong sense that justice is a relational practice through which human communities learn more of the deep truth about themselves, their nature, and their value. In a world where fake news risks undermining both justice and truth, the natural law tradition (for all its difficulties) reminds us that – at least in part – we discover truth through observing the world around us and searching for the truth as we become conscious actors in that world.

The twenty-first century is already one of extraordinary interconnection and particularity. For this reason among others, we will need a greater sense of subsidiarity, with local communities working out responsible practices on one hand and, on the other, robust, trustworthy international institutions that can monitor our moral 'bottom lines'. The UN, for example, surely remains one very important 'indispensable element in the management of world interdependence', despite its shortcomings.[52] But we must also monitor our local and individual practices, our domestic policy and the habits and assumptions which shape our everyday lives.

In the years to come, our politicians will need to think much more explicitly about the 'bilingual dialogue' between an objective and subjective sense of human rights. How do the rights of the individual harmonise with the common good? How does justice for the environment, for our common home, relate to human rights and responsibility? Religious groups have an important role to play here, articulating common features of justice and human dignity, if only we can get both language and tone right. Pope Francis's two encyclicals *Laudato si'* and *Fratelli tutti* offer significant insights into how these conversations can be conducted holistically. Pope Francis encourages us to move beyond the world of 'associates', where we encounter one another solely as partners in the pursuit of particular interests, and instead to build the solidarity that leads to genuine social friendship.[53] This kind of language, which enables a rich tapestry of human interdependence to emerge not dependent on commercial, cultural, or other indicators, is rooted in a celebration of nature itself, where 'everything is interconnected... [and which] invites us to develop a spirituality of that global solidarity which flows from the mystery of the Trinity'.[54] These two papal documents, of course, speak in explicitly Christian terms but, in both, Pope Francis is clear that he speaks to those of other faiths as well as to all people of goodwill. The task is urgent, and it is one of justice.

So, we end where we began. The social critic Ivan Illich describes the lawyer's question 'Who is my neighbour?'

in the parable of the Good Samaritan as 'a primal yearning for the intimation of limits'. The search for limits is a particularly human one, but perhaps justice has fewer hard borders if equity always encourages us to ensure that justice is rooted in truth and charity.[55] As Illich's disciple Charles Taylor puts it in his magnum opus *A Secular Age*, 'Codes, even the best codes, can become idolatrous traps...'[56] Justice is embodied in respectful, charitable relationships, underpinned by truth and equity. In the Lord's Prayer, Jesus tells his followers to pray 'Forgive us our trespasses as we forgive those who trespass against us': unless justice is done to the people I engage with, I cannot receive it myself.

# Can Institutions Be Just?

*Claire Foster-Gilbert*

In the previous essay, my esteemed colleague James Hawkey cited a speech by Martin Luther King Jr about the Good Samaritan. It was the Good Samaritan who acted justly, because he responded to the immediate and real need of the one who had fallen among thieves on the road from Jericho to Jerusalem. The priest and the Levite, meanwhile, who had passed by on the other side, were in all probability on their way to a meeting of the Jericho Road Improvement Association, thought King – and not approvingly. In this essay on institutions, it seems to me that I am making the case for the Jericho Road Improvement Association, and what a thankless, seemingly impossible task that is likely to be. From the story of the Good Samaritan onwards, we have regarded institutions with suspicion, as instruments of dehumanising policies that treat human beings as numbers, that are intent only on achieving targets that become ends in themselves, forgetting the human being at the heart of the original intention of the institution.

Speaking at a seminar in Southwark in 2018, a solicitor who represents asylum seekers observed, 'The people who work at the Home Office are decent, well-meaning, moral people. Of that, I have no doubt. But the Home Office, the institution, is my enemy.' In her words and her demeanour, the solicitor showed how alive she was to the often heart-rending human reality of each asylum seeker's story. She introduced us to one of her former clients who had managed to make a life for herself in the UK, contributing to the community and the economy, and who was pleading for recognition of her humanity rather than her status as one of millions of unwanted refugees who, to the Home Office, it seemed, were not really human.

In the parable, we are clearly to take the actions of the Good Samaritan, not those of the passers-by, as our guide. We are to tend the suffering man's wounds, to take him to a place of rest and security, and to commit ourselves to funding his long-term care. That is how we should respond to our neighbours – friends and enemies alike. The response is unconditional. There is no careful calculation of how far finite resources might go, or attempt at sharing them out equally with all. The Good Samaritan cares wholeheartedly for the one who presents his need to him. The response is utterly local, particular, personal, relational, and for all those reasons deeply human.

By means of an unforgettable caricature – the character Mrs Jellyby in *Bleak House* – Charles Dickens clearly imparts the warning of missing the need that is before us while attending to the great and grand injustices of the world. He introduces Mrs Jellyby in a chapter appropriately entitled 'Telescopic Philanthropy'. Her fervent supporter, Mr Kenge, declares:

> [Mrs Jellyby] is a lady of very remarkable strength of character, who devotes herself to the public. She has devoted herself to an extensive variety of public subjects at various times, and is, at present, until something else attracts her, devoted to the subject of Africa, with a view to the general cultivation of the coffee berry, and the natives, and the happy settlement on the banks of the African rivers of our superabundant home population.[57]

Mrs Jellyby's eyes, Dickens tells his readers, have a curious habit of seeming to look a long way off, as if they could see nothing nearer than Africa. Meanwhile, the children in the Jellyby household run amok, the servants are drunk, and Mr Jellyby spends his time sitting in a corner with his head against the wall, as if he were subject to low spirits. 'He is,' says Mr Kenge, 'merged – Merged – in the more shining qualities of his wife.'[58] I can't help feeling that Dickens would hardly complain were the reverse to be the case, with Mrs Jellyby merged in the shining qualities of her husband, whose philanthropy concentrated on far-flung fields rather than the needs of his household. Dickens would, true to the context of his nineteenth-century world, presumably have still blamed the neglect of home and family on Mrs Jellyby, and left Mr Jellyby to his wider perspective. Setting aside misogyny, however, the point of the character is to show that such concern with public subjects, with justice in general, not only misses the injustice being perpetrated very particularly under one's nose, but also often misses the mark of what would best help others. Settle our 'superabundant' population on the banks of African rivers, indeed: there's a neat policy to address Britain's alleged overcrowding. Mrs Jellyby attends to abstract problems, which is what Africa is to her, while her far-seeing eyes cannot shorten their gaze to the real people and the real problems in her own home.

In autumn 2018, at the symposium we held as part of our programme Embracing Global Challenges, then MP Rory Stewart spoke of the phenomenal institutional and intellectual weight that was brought to bear on the challenge of Afghanistan over very many years, all to no lasting avail. He argued that rather than trying to organise theoretically rational responses to such problematic cases, we – all of humanity, not just governments and charities – should do what we can. Not what we think we ought to do, because we so often get that wrong, but what we can. His counsel was not a soft option, based on observation from a distance; he had spent time in Afghanistan and had been closely involved in attempts to solve, or at least manage, the situation, and this was his authoritative conclusion.

To press the point home about the difficulty of making a case for the Jericho Road Improvement Association, I offer two real life examples, in other contexts, of what Rory Stewart might have meant. After the 2004 tsunami that devastated the countries around the Indian Ocean, Peter Browne, a neighbour in the village where I used to live, who is pathologically distrustful of institutions, decided that Something Needed To Be Done. No large-scale charity or government department could be trusted to spend our donated monies well, he believed, so he got up a fund within our little village of 200 souls and took the money himself to a village of a similar size in Sri Lanka. Working with the locals, he provided immediate relief, then funded the rebuilding of their destroyed fishing boats and provided sewing machines for the women and musical instruments for the children.

My second example is somewhat closer to home. Until a relatively short time ago, Salford was among the most deprived boroughs of Greater Manchester. Its high-rise blocks of flats were drenched in the hopelessness of their residents. The local vicar, Canon David Wyatt, fought to save his Victorian church from demolition, arguing that it was the only beautiful building left in the area. The vicar abandoned neither his church building nor the people of Salford: he is still in post and thoroughly embedded in the community. He has found endless ways of making things a bit better for the people among whom he lives. He prevented the vandalism of his church and the theft of the lead on its roof by persuading the youths embarking on their rampage to become his choir. He sat down with the most troubled boy on the block and asked him, 'Why are you so unhappy?' The boy said, 'It's all this concrete.' The vicar said, 'Let's, you and I, dig a garden.' And, between them, they did, surrounding the vicarage with green grass; flowers, and shrubs. The boy went on to become a landscape gardener and to play competitive rugby. Meanwhile, the caretaker of one of the aforesaid blocks of flats, Pear Tree Court, which overlooks the vicarage, said to herself, 'If the vicar can have a garden, I can have a pear tree orchard.' Over time, through this caretaker's determination and with the support of the vicar, the block went from being the most run-down and deprived in the area to the one with the longest waiting list. It planted its pear tree orchard, as well as a wild garden, and created a pond, and a conservatory extending out from the front door so that the more senior residents could sit in comfort and watch the wildlife proliferate under their contented gaze.

When the little local Salford flowering was brought to the attention of the bishop, he visited, and all energies dropped as he tried to make sense of the success by reference to the 'formula' it manifested. If he could get the formula clear in his head, he reasoned, then he could apply it to all the parishes in his diocese. It was a matter of institutionalising the approach, because it wasn't fair that one parish flourished when others failed. That was a postcode lottery. And yet his attempts to formalise the approach – which one could argue, and he certainly did argue, served justice – had the fairly instant effect of killing its inspiration. Thus, might the bishop have thought if he had observed the actions of the Good Samaritan, what had the Good Samaritan done that was so right that could be multiplied out and offered, with equal success, to all the others who had fallen among thieves on the Jericho Road? For if what he did could not be so multiplied, how was justice being served? And how could it be that just one tiny village in Sri Lanka received so much detailed and appropriate attention, when the millions of others around the Indian Ocean did not? And yet, how could international agencies, seeking to serve the needs of all, not just some, offer the kind of detailed, person-centred, human support that Peter Browne offered?

Making the case for the Jericho Road Improvement Association is not easy. Institutions do not elicit the energy, excitement, recognition, feeling of making a difference, and expressions of unconditional love that arise from the single-hearted response to the injustice being perpetrated before my eyes. Often the institution, the attempt to rationalise the way we act justly or care about each other, is the very means by which that care is denied or undermined. Often it seems that institutions have their members serving not justice but the institution itself.

But justice cannot do without institutions. Although I do not deny the moral beauty and value of the individual heroic act of compassion, the individual cannot bring about justice on their own. A single act of compassionate service is a good and human act, and nothing should detract from its moral value, but we cannot allow the poor, the weak, the vulnerable, and the dying to depend upon individual acts of goodwill alone.

Here is a story of a modern-day Good Samaritan who saw the need for an institution. David Nott has, for decades now, taken himself to the most dangerous areas of the world, where general and traumatic surgery is desperately needed because of conflict or natural disasters. Nott will perform life-saving surgery under terrifying conditions. He is, by any account, a hero. He has the knack, when finding himself in a situation of overwhelming need, of attending fully to the patient under his hand and seeking to save that person's life – not worrying, at that moment, about the numerous others who are also dying from lack of surgical attention. In this way, his focus and energy are not dissipated, and the one under his surgeon's knife has the best chance possible of survival.

However, Nott became only too aware of the failings of this approach. He was, of course, unable to tend to everyone who was brought to him. More tellingly, and with admirable honesty and self-awareness, he acknowledged how he felt in himself: the treacherous delight of the adrenaline rush, the feeling of being utterly needed, of his actions making the most enormous difference, of the power of saving even just one life, of being in the most dangerous situation imaginable. And he saw, even as it happened to him, the danger of burnout through exhaustion and the psychological damage from the terrible scenes he witnessed and within which he enacted his life-saving work. He saw that he had not just to perform life-saving surgery himself but to teach others how to do so. Very quickly, courses were established, and now the David Nott Foundation funds doctors from war-torn or natural-disaster-laden regions to learn the essential skills for treating people in traumatic situations. Nott, the modern embodiment of the Good Samaritan, will say that you have to go from the individual heroic act to the generalised, institutionalised application of the good you can do, otherwise justice is not served.

Nott's practical discovery is supported by the academic lawyer Kok-Chor Tan, among many others.[59] Tan argues that justice can only be realised by institutions, never by individuals. Without just institutions setting the context for action, individuals cannot on their own know how to respond to injustice. By Tan's account, institutions are not merely instrumental in bringing about justice: they are constitutive of it. Through institutions, we understand what we are entitled to and what our responsibilities are. Just institutions remove the dependence of the vulnerable on the goodwill of the wealthy, and they relieve the individual of the burden of knowing they will never be able to serve everyone's needs.

The creation of circuit judges in the twelfth century by Henry II brought into being a just institution, which ensured that the law became the law of the land, the common law. The circuit judges were responsible for administering, across the realm, the law that was made in Westminster. Within a just legal system, judges can attend to each case brought before them without, in that moment, having to worry about all the other cases (that is, live cases rather than previous cases which set precedent that must be taken into account in every case). The judge's duty, assigned by the institution, is to administer justice here, now, in this court. Their energy and focus are not dissipated. Similarly, physicians are freed, by the NHS, from the paralysing awareness of the size and complexity of all the healthcare needs in the country. They can tend to each patient before them wholeheartedly. Police officers can deal with the specific crime to which they are called. Civil servants can attend to their bit of policy, and so on. And we can volunteer individual acts of self-sacrifice and service, which come from deep altruistic motives, to our heart's content, without worrying that the poor will suffer because our urge to help may not be sustainable. And we can recognise, learning with due humility from the lesson of Mrs Jellyby, that our acts of compassion serve to maintain our own moral health and sense of well-being, as well as benefiting others.

Just institutions give a context to our individual attempts to serve and locate them within a greater narrative of service. Just institutions are the means by which humans can work with each other, uniting our efforts, creating something that is greater than the sum of its parts, reducing the chance of actions clashing with each other or cancelling each other out. We have, then, a moral duty to ensure our institutions are just. Sometimes we have a moral duty to create new just institutions, as, for example, the UN was created in 1945.

I believe a new just institution is needed now to serve ecological justice. Though we have little enough time to address the ecological crisis, the mode of our response is more akin to a marathon than a sprint. Human compassion runs out of steam if every just act depends solely upon it. News headlines are voracious in their need for new subjects; they can't just keep shouting 'We're all doomed'. Activism must reinvent itself again and again, and individuals, even growing collections of individuals, cannot keep doing this. There is so much to do, and every human being has a part to play, so an institutional response is the best way to ensure the necessary efforts are demanded of us and sustained. The ecological cause is just and long-lasting, as the mobilisation of schoolchildren by Greta Thunberg showed, but even their weekly truancy to make the point could not be sustained.

There can be tremendous excitement at the creation of a new institution. The cause it has been founded to serve is, at last, being taken seriously. The new institution commands resources and strategy, channels goodwill; there is a sense of direction and moral purpose. Above all, there is energy. The contrast could not be greater between this novel institutional energy and the apparently moribund, apparently no longer just, old institutions that cease to energise, that kill off inspiration, silence the spirit of compassion and humanity, serve themselves and not the cause they were created for, absorb money and attention, are morally corroded. It is tempting to look at them and decide to destroy them, to start again, especially as we believe we would know how to create a better institution today. 'Our rubbish Parliament,' we think, 'taking up so much time on a Brexit deal that no one wants and producing confusing COVID rules.' 'Our rubbish civil service, turning people into numbers, and implementing policies that only work in theory.' 'Our rubbish judiciary, the "enemies of the people", ignoring the democratic mandate of a referendum.'

But these are lazy caricatures based upon misdirected anger. We are lucky to have a constitutional balance of power in the UK that, at its heart, serves justice. A balance that is struck between the democratic responsibility and final accountability of the MP who is elected to represent local constituents; of the civil servant, bound by honesty, integrity, political impartiality, and objectivity; of the judge, bound to uphold the rule of law without fear or favour. The institutions of the legislature, the executive, and the judiciary are, in essence, the custodians of justice, vital components of a civilised society. But that does not mean that the institutions are anywhere near perfect servants of justice. It is not feasible to suggest that there will ever be a time when they are, just as we will never see moral perfection in ourselves. Rather, we might see them as being better, or worse, at responding to the call of justice. Imagine the institutions as boats, sailing through water. In the analogy, justice is the compass point, setting the direction of travel. It is that towards which the institutions are journeying, that by which they are called. And, as all good skippers know, you cannot fix your helm rigidly but must constantly adjust it in response to the wind and waves. Your skill is in keeping the boat no more than five degrees either side of the compass point towards which you are travelling, even as it navigates its way through sometimes choppy waters and unfavourable winds.

There are three threats to institutions' abilities to sail in the direction of justice. First, they can set up systems that fail to serve the just purpose for which they were created, taking the boat right off course. Second, they can expend more energy in maintaining themselves than in delivering the service they are intended to offer, endlessly polishing the brass fittings and scrubbing the deck. Third, they can become morally corroded and corrupted, with the crew deliberately jeopardising the journey from motives of self-interest.

The first threat, that institutional systems do not serve justice even if the institution itself claims to, can be seen historically. The House of Commons, for example, once represented only some of the population – variously landowners, then most men, then women over the age of thirty and so on, meaning universal franchise is still under 100 years old. Only 150 years ago, the civil service was populated by means of patronage, not merit. And 1,000 years ago, there was no mechanism to ensure the law was applied equally across the land. But although those historic injustices have been addressed, we cannot cease to keep watch. Institutional struggles can be felt today as, for example, politicians interpret their democratic mandate differently by choosing different loyalties: their constituents; their parliamentary party; or their conscience. Civil servants wrestle with the challenge of avoiding postcode lotteries in health, education, housing, and immigration, while not turning people into numbers. Judges face a lack of resources, especially in the availability of legal aid, and the consequent inequality of access to the courts. There are certainly many institutional injustices of which we are simply unaware. It is a telling example of how we can think we are just while colluding in injustice, that equality before the law has only at the end of the twentieth century been taken to mean that no regard should be paid to a person's gender, ethnicity, or sexual orientation. Even so, we are being made more and more aware of institutional bias. The work towards justice in institutions can never be declared finished, but the struggles are made within still-venerable institutions and they are, on the whole, *towards* justice, not away from it. Justice remains the navigation point.

Here is a wincingly awful, possibly apocryphal story that illustrates the second threat, that the institution itself will absorb more energy than it expends on the justice it should be serving. When the Department for the Environment occupied three tower blocks in Marsham Street, now demolished, there was a civil servant whose sole job was to assign offices as their colleagues' seniority changed, with their pencil allocating new offices and their razor blade erasing old ones, all day, every day.[60] Today, arguably, the opposite danger is the case: that not enough resource and support is given to those who tend the ecology of government, Parliament, and the judiciary, ensuring the department, debating chamber, or court is running as it should be.

The third threat, of internal corrosion and corruption, is always present. Virtuous institutions – that is, ones that have been created to further good causes, like justice – can be caught out if the assumption is made that, since virtue is the goal of the institution, virtue will, inevitably, be its character. It was, I confess, a shock to arrive at the headquarters of the Church of England and find there all the human failings I had known in myself and my colleagues in the secular law school at King's College London. It shocked us all to find Oxfam employees exploiting women while ostensibly serving countries in great need. The MPs' expenses scandal stayed in the headlines for weeks on end back in 2009 because it was thankfully hard to believe that our elected representatives could fiddle the books in this way, and more recent allegations of bullying and sexual harassment are similarly scandalous. Institutional anti-Semitism and Islamophobia are alleged and, in some cases, proved. Institutions that serve good ends have to pay great attention to the ethos that prevails within them. Just because you are responsible for trying to ensure the citizens of the UK are, say, adequately housed – unquestionably a just cause – it does not mean that your personal receipts are beneath your notice, nor that you are no longer required to be courteous to your staff. Writing staff policies and creating yet more oversight committees will not address moral corrosion. The heads, hearts, and actions of the people in the institution have to be engaged too.

I have argued that we cannot have justice without just institutions, and I have suggested ways in which the justice of institutions can be threatened. Running like a thread through these matters is the presence of human agency. For although institutions undoubtedly take on lives of their own, they are what they are because of the people who work in them and the people for whom they were created. And this observation brings me back to the Good Samaritan.

I am not going to conclude my essay by suggesting that Jesus was wrong to champion the actions of the Good Samaritan. The just act of one person is powerful. Nott, our contemporary Good Samaritan, knew from a utilitarian perspective that his individual services as a surgeon in places of conflict were pretty futile. But that did not stop him from going to those places, nor did it stop him from focusing on the person in front of him, doing everything he could to save that life. It was what he was called to do. The navigation point of justice for him drew him in this very particular direction, and his individual focus was supported by the Talmudic saying that 'whoever saves one life, saves the whole world'.[61] Because he wasn't paralysed by the size of the problem, as a utilitarian might have been, some lives were saved that would not otherwise have been. But there was another, unmeasurable outcome to his precise and particular individual service, which made an enormous difference: saving one life boosted the morale of the whole team and gave them all more courage and energy to continue to do what they could. A similar effect is observable when NHS staff applaud as one patient whose life they have saved from COVID-19 departs from their hospital. Everyone takes heart from single successes in bleak times. This power of individual agency means that if you think you are operating within an institution that was created to serve justice but isn't managing very well, either in the way it promotes overly utilitarian policies or in the institution-alised, unjust attitudes of its staff, it is still important that you yourself try to respond to the call of justice and model just behaviour. You will be attractive to people of goodwill and, if the institution is dedicated to serving justice, as I believe our public service institutions still are, then your example will count, and the power of good-ness itself will come and support you.

I close with a story told to me by a Hindu friend. A little bird found, to her horror, that the ocean had swept over her nest and taken her eggs. She stood on the sea-shore and cried to the waves, 'Give them back! Give my eggs back!' The ocean ignored her; the waves ebbed and flowed; the water continued to cover and hold back her eggs. She cried and cried to no avail. But, instead of giving up, determination grew in her, the fierce love of a mother refusing to surrender her offspring to the cruel sea. If the sea would not return her eggs, she decided, then she would empty the sea. She flew up, dived down towards the water, and took a drop of the sea into her beak. She flew back to the shore and let the drop of sea-water fall. Back she flew to the sea, took a drop of water in her beak, flew back to the land and dropped the drop of water. Back to the sea, a drop of its water, back to the land, letting loose the drop. Back to the sea, back to the land, back and forth, a hundred times, a thousand times. As night fell, she wearily continued, her determination to empty the sea unabated. In the early morning, she was still flying back and forth. Her single drops amounted to no more than a cupful, but still she worked. Finally, the god of the sea, who had been watching, could bear it no more. He went to her and said,

'What are you trying to do?'

'I'm emptying the ocean,' she replied.

'Why?'

'Because the ocean has stolen my eggs and won't give them back.'

'But you will never empty the ocean.'

'Never?'

'It will take you a thousand years.'

'Then I will take a thousand years, but I will not give up.'

The god took pity on her and commanded the ocean to return her eggs.

## Audience member

I wonder whether you could say something more about institutions that have become time-honoured and have fallen prey to all three problems you discuss. How do they begin to renew themselves? And how does David Nott, who is trying to institutionalise what he is doing as a Good Samaritan by setting up the David Nott Foundation, retain the individual Good Samaritan ethos within an institution, and keep renewing it?

## Claire Foster-Gilbert

It doesn't happen by itself. Leaders within institutions need to attend to it. For example, Jonathan Evans, the Director General of the Security Service, decided that he should maintain what he called 'ethical buoyancy' in his institution by appointing an ethics counsellor to whom all the operatives had access. They could speak in confidence about any concerns they might have. He realised that the operatives in MI5 are both its greatest strength and its greatest weakness, and so addressing ethical concerns directly with them was the best way to ensure his institution was just. Westminster Abbey Institute provides opportunities for public service institutions to recalibrate, to allow their members to reconnect with the vocation of public service. My experience with the Institute has been that this recalibration doesn't take very long, because the vocation is not far beneath the skin of most public servants; it just gets forgotten, or it gets dusty, or covered over with being too busy. Creating the opportunity to reconnect and recalibrate to the heart of one's calling, and the calling of one's institution, is very important. The structural injustices are always present too. We should constantly ask the question: what injustice is built into the systems of my institution that I am not seeing? Diverse perspectives are critical to that self-interrogation. This work has to be done deliberately.

**Audience member**
What can everyday people do to help ensure just institutions? What can all of us do, today, to strengthen our institutions and help them become more just?

**Claire Foster-Gilbert**
To quote Rory Stewart again: do what you can, and see that it is connected to a wider effort. You and I are not the heroes, the saviours of the world, but there will be something you are good at, that you love doing, that sets your belly on fire, that you can pursue. It will be something

good, that serves others. It won't be making money: we know from research that after making a certain amount of money (and it's not very much), money has no relation to happiness at all. Your effort will be sustained if it's towards something good. And do what you can to support the good in existing just institutions. I had a conversation with a young doctor recently, who told me, 'I always used to vote, but I've given up. I mean, who would I vote for?' I said he had to carry on voting, however difficult the choices. You have to keep voting for the sake of democracy. Don't let us lose faith in these institutions.

**Audience member**
When you find canker in the centre of apparently virtuous institutions – Oxfam, Save the Children, the Church – what should the public approach be? Should they stop giving money to Oxfam, for instance?

**Claire Foster-Gilbert**
When I came to work for the Church of England, I found some really, really bad behaviour was justified because our goal was to establish the kingdom of heaven. The ends apparently justified the means. But they don't. Of course the goals of your institution are important; they are the reason for the institution's existence. You

must think about whether those goals are just, but you must also think about how you're going to achieve those goals and whether the actions you undertake to do so are, in and of themselves, morally acceptable or not. It doesn't matter how great the goal is: if the action is harming people, or involves lying, covering up, or exploitation, the action is wrong. The goal does not justify bad behaviour. Moreover, wrong actions in service of a good goal corrupt the goal. And you should not just establish good goals and good ways to reach those goals, you should also check that the good you are seeking to do is what is wanted. Charities and the Church can get very big for their boots, thinking they know what's best for other people, and that's not necessarily true.

**Audience member**

My mind goes back to the film *I, Daniel Blake*. I can picture the Jobcentre and the Jobcentre worker who had to turn away Daniel Blake. How can your philosophy have an impact at that micro level? We can talk, today, about the austerity that is affecting so many people unseen. They're not here, in these illustrious, great places; they're alone in small places with no power, with no speech, with no one to represent them.

## Claire Foster-Gilbert

Part of an answer to your question is that the people on the front line should have delegated authority. A police officer has the most extraordinary amount of power: the power of arrest. They are called to deal with a disturbance, and they have to analyse sometimes highly complex circumstances, where there may be emotional or physical abuse within a family or neighbourhood, abuse of drugs or alcohol, histories of mental ill-health: enough complexity to keep a moral philosopher busy for ten years. The police officer has to deal with all of it, and quickly. They're not always going to get it right, but they'll do their best, and it helps to know that you have the confidence of your institution behind you. With your leaders properly delegating authority to you on the front line, and supporting you, you are much more likely to make a wise decision. It goes without saying that you should come to that situation adequately trained. The same is true of all front-line staff, because they are the ones who have the human, face-to-face encounter; the people in Whitehall don't have that. But the people in Whitehall are understanding this difference better and better. It's an ongoing challenge to create a system that is just and equal across the country but that also empowers the face-to-face encounter, where the actual knowledge of the need is.

**Audience member**

I'd like to ask a question about the link, or potential link, between democracy and just institutions. There's been a move, over the last five, six years or so, to introduce more democratically elected leaders to institutions, whether for police and crime commissioners or elected local mayors. Do you think that that level of democracy aids an institution?

**Claire Foster-Gilbert**

As one of the Institute Fellows said to me: there is nothing like the feeling of representing the people who have voted for you; nothing. I haven't met an MP yet who doesn't feel an almost sacred responsibility for their constituents. Every citizen in the UK should feel connected to somebody who represents them in Parliament, because everybody has an MP. But democracy is a volatile beast. If you are democratically elected, you have to attend to power, because it is being elected into power that gives you the mandate to serve. Walking alongside you, as you try to make the world a better place, is the morally corrosive demand that power makes on you: will this decision or this action serve to keep me in power or not? MPs should be thoroughly aware of their susceptibility to moral corrosion simply by the nature of democracy. They are also protected by the British constitution, which supports democracy through a politically impartial civil service, an independent judiciary, and, dare I say it, some fairly intelligent contributions from the House of Lords. Making a role subject to democratic election increases accountability but it also opens it to the corrosive effect of power-seeking, so that role must have in place the support of those who are independent of it, non-political people who are unafraid to speak truth to power.

**Audience member**
I work in the Department for International Development. It's a very vocational department, but there are occasionally tensions between what individual civil servants think is the right thing to do and the corporate position. I want some practical advice on what leaders should do to stimulate a debate about speaking truth to power, but also working out, for an individual, how to sit with their conscience and do the job that the corporate body is saying we've got to do.

**Claire Foster-Gilbert**
To manage that relationship is the challenge of anybody within any institution. I would say, beware moral certainty. Beware the thought that you and you alone know what is right, and everybody else has got it wrong. You

may be right, that may be the case, but just beware, if you're absolutely certain, because there's likely to be something you haven't thought of. The world is a messy place, as civil servants in the Department for International Development would know better than most, and we are doing the best we can. And the glory and the challenge and the pain of working with other people is that you have to compromise. It'd be easy if you were on your own, just making your own decisions, and nobody else was affected and nobody else had a view, but – thank heavens, because you'd get it wrong – it's not the case, and a good institution will find a way of holding the differences and moving forward nevertheless. Voting is one way to deal with disagreement, if you have a good, just system of voting and people believe in the system and can accept losing as well as winning. That's one way of doing it. But often with moral decisions a vote isn't the way. It's not binary, you know; everybody needs help in thinking through an issue. You want to have a proper discussion and explore the questions without fear of being thought stupid or having the wrong view or being penalised for going against the corporate view. That is for leaders to create: the atmosphere within which it's possible to have that kind of learning conversation, everybody recognising that we work this out together, and not everybody is going to be happy all the time. It isn't just a matter of gathering a group of people in a room and taking their views. My view is always changing, and I want help in working out what is the right thing to do. I'm not just somebody 'with a view' that is either ignored or accepted. It's much more interesting than that, and nuanced, and compromising.

# Is a Just Society Possible?

*Jane Sinclair*

The world is manifestly an unjust place.

Professor Alexis Jay's report on systematic sexual abuse in Rotherham was published in August 2014. The Jay Report findings were horrific. Fourteen hundred mainly white girls and young women had been sexually abused, and in some instances tortured, in and around Rotherham over a period of twenty or so years, predominantly by British-Pakistani men. Prosecutions followed Jay's revelations, and, by March 2019, nineteen men and two women had received prison sentences for the abuse for which they were responsible, some of it dating back to the 1980s. One of the ringleaders was imprisoned for thirty-five years.

All of this is well documented alongside sadly similar patterns of abuse in a number of other British towns and cities. But what made the Rotherham situation particularly shocking was the failure of local community leaders – from both Rotherham Metropolitan Borough Council

(RMBC) and South Yorkshire Police – to act on reports of this abuse, made over many years prior to 2010. Some of the survivors attempted to make reports of abusive behaviour directly to the police. They were ignored. The charity Risky Behaviour was set up by RMBC in 1997 to work with girls and women aged eleven to twenty-five who were thought to be at risk of sexual exploitation on the streets of the town. A youth worker, Jayne Senior, was the project coordinator from 1999 to 2002. Senior found evidence of what appeared to be an organised local grooming network in Rotherham. Such was the quantity of her evidence, including reports from many victims of abuse, that Senior was advised by the police to forward her evidence to an electronic 'drop box' on the South Yorkshire Police computer system. She later learned that the police had not read the reports she had left there and that the information could not be accessed by other forces. RMBC itself came to view Risky Business as a nuisance, and the project was shut down by the council in 2011.

Senior eventually published her own account of what she had experienced and learnt in Rotherham.[62] Further official reports into the failure of RMBC to deal appropriately with reports of abuse over many years have been published, not least by Dame Louise Casey.[63]

I served as Vicar of Rotherham during the period

2003 to 2007, when this abuse was at its height. I knew nothing of it then. It suited the perpetrators – and, apparently, the council and South Yorkshire Police – not to talk about what was happening, but I was familiar with the town's culture and the social and moral assumptions that enabled the abuse to flourish.

Rotherham is a metropolitan borough of some quarter of a million people, mainly white but with significant British-Pakistani and some other smaller British-Asian communities. It's a very mixed place, with pockets of deep deprivation alongside more prosperous working- and middle-class areas. All ages are represented among its population, and the town and its satellite communities have all the amenities you would expect for a borough of its size. It has had to deal with significant challenges since the 1970s, not least the closure of the coal mines and the reorganisation of the steel industry. Jobs and job opportunities have changed, but Rotherham is not untypical of many South Yorkshire towns with a resilient, down-to-earth population, the vast majority of whom are good, well-meaning citizens who care passionately for their community and want to see the town and their neighbourhood and their own families flourish.

Yet, behind all this, the Jay Report revealed sinister, systematic abuse that had gone unchecked despite multiple opportunities. The failure to address the abuse was subsequently attributed to a number of factors including race, class, and gender. To put it simply, no action was taken because of cultural assumptions, fears, and a corporate blindness on the part of the town's leadership and in the wider community.[64]

To illustrate: in Rotherham, contemptuous and sexist attitudes were commonly expressed towards the mainly working-class girls who were abused. The language used by some, across all ethnicities, was telling. Girls and young women who hung around taxis or the clubs in the town centre were often called 'sluts' or 'trash'. They were assumed to be 'easy meat' out for drugs or alcohol or sex because 'that is what they wanted'. Those who were abused were simply not believed when they spoke of being victims; they were treated with contempt. The girls' and women's human dignity was denied in the very language used to speak of them.

Injustice flourished unchecked for far too long in Rotherham. Sadly, the town's reputation was shattered and will take years to recover. The cost of this injustice has been huge, global even, in its reach: the white supremacist and convicted mass murderer Brenton Tarrant daubed the name 'Rotherham' on one of the magazines of bullets he used in the mosque massacres in Christchurch, New Zealand in March 2019.

But injustice in society is not confined to obvious cases of the abuse of the vulnerable. Opportunities for good education; the possibility of earning a living wage; fair access to means of legal redress and to decent health-care; and freedom from slavery, social oppression, and the threat of violence: by almost any measure of what is necessary to be able to flourish in UK society, 30 per cent or more of those under the age of eighteen in the UK are the unintended and unwilling victims of an unjust distribution of opportunity and wealth when compared with the remaining 70 per cent of their contemporaries.[65] The same case could be made for many other vulnerable social groups: the elderly; those with disabilities; those who experience homelessness. All of these groups face the day-to-day consequences of inadequate social provision and limited freedom of choice.

The experience of actual or perceived injustice is not even limited to the least well-off or the most vulnerable in society. How often do we hear spouses in the midst of divorce proceedings complaining bitterly about the 'unfair division', as they see it, of their assets? Never mind what the law says or what the children require by way of support, the partner with the greater assets frequently resents the 'injustice' of having to relinquish substantial assets to the other party.

Most visions of a just society, at least in Western,

broadly liberal social traditions, might be said to be based on ideas of common human dignity and value, of truthfulness, hope, a belief that social and individual change for the better is possible, underpinned by freedom of speech, equality of opportunity, and the rule of law as guardians of those ideas. These values are given expression in the Universal Declaration of Human Rights.[66] While not using the word 'justice' within its text, the declaration spells out the basic rights – such as the right to life and freedom from slavery and torture – that many would argue are essential markers of a just society. Because a properly just society is a society in which relationships between individuals, communities, institutions, and nations are rightly ordered; where human dignity and value are celebrated; where all citizens have the opportunity to participate in the government of their community and nation; where all have equal opportunity to access education, healthcare, and the law; where goods, housing, and pay are available according to need; where diversity is acknowledged as a strength; where freedom of speech and belief are norms; where human flourishing, in all its diversity, is possible.

Despite some well-documented failures, these characteristics may be observed in much of British society today. British citizens have the opportunity to participate in the government of their communities, both locally and nationally. Our electoral system is well run, and it is guarded by laws that are enforceable.[67] Virtually all children resident in the UK have access to a good education. We have a National Health Service which, though it may always be under pressure – especially during the COVID-19 pandemic – is in essence available to all and free at their point of need. The principles that underpin British society are consonant with generally accepted values of social justice. But British society is not perfectly just. There do appear to be some yawning chasms between the reality in which we live and our aspirations to live in a more just society.

Among many issues, there are at least four major challenges that need to be addressed if a more just society is to be established in the UK.

The first challenge is that of human nature itself. The philosopher Thomas Hobbes famously observed that life outside society would be 'solitary, poor, nasty, brutish, and short'.[68] In Hobbes's view, 'human beings are all basically selfish, driven by fear of death and the hope of personal gain'. He argues that all of us seek power over others, whether we realise this or not. This may seem to be an unduly pessimistic view of human nature, but we all live as if this pessimistic view is true. If you do not accept Hobbes's picture of humanity, why do you lock the door when you leave your house? Presumably it is because you think there are people out there who would happily steal everything you own. On Hobbes's terms, and perhaps ours, only the rule of law and the threat of punishment keep us in check. Indeed, whether or not we agree wholeheartedly with Hobbes, it is certainly true that the majority of us are inclined to act from mixed motives much of the time.

Seeking a more just society is something to which many of us aspire, but there are competing claims on our attention and resources. Which comes first: my pay rise, so that I can feed my family well, or ensuring that someone who has no job receives sufficient benefits on which to live? Should a baby have specialist care that could extend her life by a few years but will cost a million pounds or more, or should the money be spent on a clinic, where detox opportunities can be offered to a hundred people addicted to drugs for the next three years? Both might be just choices, but on what grounds is a just choice to be made?

At worst, we can be so focused on our own or our family's survival – on our rights, cares, and personal responsibilities – that we simply ignore any consideration of the wider good of the community or society of which we are a part. In that sense, we can be described as Darwinian. We are animals, wired to ensure our personal survival. The cynic might argue that what passes for so-called altruistic behaviour on our part is often for our own benefit, the benefit of others being a fortunate by-product. For example, I might choose to direct all my charitable giving to the local hospice, where, in the fullness of time, I might expect to end my own days. I am looking after others now, but with an eye to my own well-being in due course.

Yet it is also characteristic of humans that we can do better than act selfishly, at least sometimes. Take people who have freely given their lives so that others might live. Famously, the Polish Roman Catholic priest Maximilian Kolbe offered to take the punishment that was being meted out to a young Jewish father in the Auschwitz concentration camp. Kolbe was placed in solitary confinement and starved for three weeks, before finally being put out of his suffering by a camp doctor, who injected him with a lethal dose of carbolic acid. The young father survived and lived to tell the tale. Working for justice – in this case, protecting the lives of others – is possible, if challenging. It can demand extraordinary courage in the face of deeply embedded instinctive behaviours.

The second challenge we face is our inheritance of unjust social structures and skewed expectations. The UK parliamentary expenses scandal first came to light in 2009. MPs had been caught on the horns of a dilemma for many years. They were responsible for deciding the level of their own pay and had come to believe, with some justification, that the electorate thought that they were overpaid. MPs, however, had to pay for their own secretarial help and other research assistance, and the figures just did not add up. The expenses system had thus come to be used as a means of topping up what MPs needed in order to undertake their work at Westminster properly. But there were no effective checks on the system, and abuses took place. Among the most scandalous examples were alleged expenses claims for a duck feeding station and cleaning a moat, alongside generous housing arrangements, all funded by the taxpayer. Public exposure, some criminal prosecutions, and attempts at a massive overhaul of the expenses system followed, with much firmer monitoring put into place. Yet at the root of it all, as well as venality on the part of some politicians, was public ignorance of the reality of MPs' working lives. We all unconsciously colluded in an inherited unjust system and then sought to shift the blame away from ourselves. The temptation to moral corrosion across society is never far away.

Our third challenge is the wide range of views over what constitutes justice or just behaviour, and conceptual differences between cultures and communities. Matters of gender and sexuality receive starkly different treatment even among communities within the UK, let alone across the globe. Andrew Moffat has taught at Parkfield Community School in Birmingham for a number of years. In 2017, he was awarded an MBE for his work on developing equality education in the school, including his development of the No Outsiders programme, which focuses on inclusion in British society. However, 98 per cent of the school's pupils are Muslim, and the programme caused outrage among some of the children's parents, who believe it is anti-Islamic. Here is a clear clash of opinion over what constitutes just behaviour. Moffat feels it's important that his pupils become familiar with current liberal British attitudes; the pupils' parents, on the other hand, feel it's important to guard their Islamic cultural norms of behaviour. Which should prevail?

And what of the cases of families keeping their children out of mainstream education and only teaching them within the very narrow confines of a particular faith, as has been the case with some madrasas, yeshivas, and fundamentalist Christian homeschoolers? Here are examples of the clash of differing views of just behaviour, of just education, and of what constitutes the provision of justice of opportunity for children.

The fourth challenge is broader still. The UK is but one nation in a global community of interdependent nation states. The need for an arena in which to resolve conflicts peacefully, and the development of what were known for many years as 'friendly relations between states', was recognised in the aftermath of the First World War. The League of Nations, set up in 1920, was short-lived. The UN has survived for longer. Its soft power, through such bodies as UNESCO and UNHCR, is still significant, but its power to enforce resolutions passed by the Security Council is virtually non-existent. With the exception of the International Court of Justice in the Hague, the international community has few institutions with the power to take effective action for the promotion of justice. With this international vacuum, it is left to superpowers – the USA, China, or Russia – to claim the moral high ground when they attempt to justify their own actions and interventions in other countries. The ability to negotiate effective treaties that might promote just behaviour between states is entirely dependent on geopolitical circumstances and national interests.

It might appear that a just society is impossible to achieve, but that does not lessen the need to work towards one.

In the previous essay, Claire Foster-Gilbert argues that a way forward might be to view justice as a direction as well as a goal, a moral compass bearing that we can seek to follow, as boats might follow a compass bearing at sea.

Consider a fundamental taproot of justice, at least as it is inherited by Western democracies and the UK in particular. The three Abrahamic faiths of Judaism, Christianity, and Islam all assert that the root of justice is divine. God's will is for all people, all creation, to exist in just relationship with itself and with God. The influence of Judaeo-Christian traditions on how we in Britain think about justice, and in particular how we shape our system of justice, continues to be profound. And in the Judaeo-Christian tradition, the activity of doing justice and the quality of being righteous go hand in hand. Righteousness is a divine attribute, implying holiness and goodness in the very best senses of those words. To be righteous is to act justly; righteousness is the quality God has, and we may have. Justice is the outworking of righteousness. And the purposes of righteousness and justice are straightforward: to mend broken relationships between God and people and between human beings, to protect the vulnerable and thus to enable all in a society to flourish.

The biblical scholar Walter Brueggemann speaks of justice as 'God's earthly form of holiness.'[69] But divine justice in the traditions of the Old Testament is not fundamentally about fairness; it is a radical notion of distributive practice that gives to each one what is needed in order to live a life of well-being. In theological terms, the God of the biblical writers is partial, prone to mercy – 'unjust' in common human parlance. The prophets give a devastating critique of Israel's social practice in their day, insisting that no wealth, power, knowledge, or privilege could make society safe, since the most elemental requirements of neighbourliness are disregarded. God's people, however, are called to care practically for the vulnerable, the stranger, and those without adequate means of support. In the Bible, this quality of righteousness is given real meaning in day-to-day commerce, familial relationships, and in the generous treatment of immigrants. All of life is meant to be geared towards just behaviour.

Underpinning these ideas is a profound notion of agreement – a covenant – between God and God's people: God will remain faithful to the people; He will protect and sustain them. The people, in turn, will give allegiance to God and act justly in all their relationships. The covenant is a type of divine social contract, which has been, and continues to be, paralleled in some of our own contractual social relationships. Those of us who are British citizens have 'contracted' relationships with the state. If you hold a British passport, you have certain rights and responsibilities as a citizen, just as the British state has responsibilities for you, especially if you are travelling overseas.

The public institutions of this country are intended to enact this contractual relationship with British citizens. At their best, these institutions seek to ensure just – though this may not mean equal – access to resources according to need. Benefits exist, in theory at least, to ensure that no one falls into absolute poverty. Unsurprisingly, these systems sometimes fail, with horrendous results. The poor implementation of Universal Credit, for example, has wreaked havoc on families and communities nationwide. But seeking to apportion blame is often unhelpful. Public servants simply do not have sufficient access to the truthful reality of how people manage their lives. Politicians are not perfect, and can enact inadequate laws, or fail to enact laws at all, to protect the vulnerable.

What might be done to begin to promote a more just society? It may be a deeply unfashionable idea, but might we work to recover a confidence in the traditional virtues – righteous virtues – of goodness, truthfulness, and humility? These are among the bedrocks of just behaviour, the markers of a just society. We lose them at our peril. When fake news reigns, when economic success at any cost is idolised, when contempt for others is broadcast far and wide on social media, when fear is puffed up into egocentric swagger, then justice withers and tyranny looms large over society. We would do well to be bold for humble, virtuous living; to cultivate patience and kindness in our personal relationships; and, in our institutional life, to enable justice to flourish in our midst. The prophet Micah puts it neatly: 'What does the Lord require of you but to do justice, to love kindness, and to walk humbly with your God?' (Micah 6:8).

The four challenges outlined earlier remain, but we might make it our business to encourage altruism, putting the needs of others first. We would need to work against our instinct for self-preservation; we would need to find the humility to learn from other cultures that are more in touch with their communal roots than we are in the West; we would need to create opportunities to meet with people very different from ourselves, and to learn to listen well.

Might we not aim to be more honest about our social inheritance and, sometimes, our skewed points of view when it comes to institutions? Perhaps we need to cultivate ways of owning up to our responsibilities and where we have failed to act to ensure that the vulnerable are protected. We need to learn how to be more alert to our own tendencies to moral corrosion.

In a multicultural society, we can easily forget our ignorance of each other, with our differing ideas about just behaviour and expectations. At the very least, getting to know our neighbour and enabling them to get to know us would be a step towards better understanding. In the end, our democratically agreed laws are what safeguard the freedoms of everyone who lives in the UK, whatever their culture. Those laws need to be understood within real, neighbourly relationships, and then observed for the sake of us all.

The establishment of effective means of developing just behaviour between peoples and nations is a long-term and seemingly impossible task at the moment, but diplomats, politicians, and all the rest of us must not give up. That way lies injustice and violence. As Foster-Gilbert reminds us: do what you can, but do not beat yourself up about what you cannot do.

People of goodwill need to be prepared to work together for justice. We need to buck the blame culture that seeks to find scapegoats whenever anything goes wrong. We should be truth-seekers, not blame-finders. This demands courage, and boldness to speak out. Those who seek to uphold our constitutional arrangements need our support. Of course, we should be critical when we believe that unjust decisions are being made in the courts, or in Parliament, or by people in public office, but then we also need to suggest positive alternatives, get involved, seek to make what changes we can for the better. A more just society is only going to come about if we seek to make it come about. We cannot afford to leave it to others.

Is a just society possible? A just society is not going to be achieved by human effort alone, which falls prey to our mixed motives and the complexities of the society in which we live. But a more just society is worth working for, nonetheless. As one rabbi memorably put it, 'God made the world unjust in order that we might work for justice.'[70] It is the direction we choose that is important. We need to be bold and to choose that moral compass of justice, whose wavering point invites us onwards together to seek the well-being of others, whatever challenges lie ahead.

Finally, a postscript to the events in Rotherham. It was widely reported in March 2019 that some of the Rotherham survivors were being compelled to disclose, in Disclosure and Barring Service checks, convictions they received when they were being abused. This happened when they applied for jobs, or even for membership of parent-teacher associations. The offences included soliciting, possessing an offensive weapon, and assault. All these were actions forced upon the survivors by their abusers. The survivors can never put their past behind them. In the process of enacting an absolutely essential law, which is intended to safeguard the most vulnerable in society, our legal system was perpetrating an act of injustice against women who were themselves survivors of abuse. For justice, we cannot rely on systems, on institutions, and on laws alone; they will always prove to be inadequate to some degree. To achieve true justice, we have to look beyond systems and laws and be prepared to look deep within ourselves.

# Notes

1   N. Simmonds, *Law as a Moral Idea* (Oxford, 2007), 63.

2   *Ibid.*

3   See M. Luther King Jr, 'I've Been to the Mountaintop', *American Rhetoric*, accessed online.

4   This narrative does not belong solely to the Christian tradition. It has also been used by secular commentators, by the Palestinian Muslim Ali Abu Awwad, and by modern Jewish thinkers. This story full of 'inverted expectations' saves us 'from the way of blood', in the words of one of our leading interfaith theologians (see J. Walters, *Loving Your Neighbour in an Age of Religious Conflict: A New Agenda for Interfaith Relations* (London, 2019) 17ff). It saves us from injustice.

5   J. Waldron, 'The Image of God: Rights, Reason and Order' in J. Witte and F. S. Alexander, eds, *Christianity and Human Rights* (Oxford, 2010), 217.

6    It's also worth pointing out that the use of
     the *imago Dei* as a foundational rock for
     the development of theories of justice is not
     entirely free from difficulties for Christians and
     Jews. What kind of image do we mean? What
     effect does sin have? How does this relate to
     contemporary explorations of the human person in
     anthropological, social, and medical spheres?

7    J. Rawls, *Political Liberalism* (New York, 1993),
     224–5.

8    'Universal Declaration of Human Rights', *United
     Nations*, 10 December 1948.

9    For the story of Smuts' preamble and the drafts
     of a new chapter, see P. Marshall, 'Smuts and the
     Preamble to the UN Charter', *The Round Table*
     (2001), 90/358, 55–65.

10   B. Williams O.P., 'Human rights: A Bilingual
     Dialogue', *Diritti umani: Problema nodale nel
     mondo contemporaneo*, Pontifical University of
     Saint Thomas Aquinas, Rome, 9 March 1988.

11   God is the *summum bonum* – the highest good.

12   *Summa Theologica* (ST) II–II:58:11.

13   ST II–II:109:1. Lying is the opposing vice to this
     virtue. He does occasionally allow, in difficult
     situations, for the concealment or withholding of
     truth, but never for negating or contradicting it.

Many commentators have argued that in so doing Thomas is upholding a principle that is vital for individual and social human flourishing.

14   ST II–II:120:2.

15   ST II–II:120:1.

16   See E. Rennie, 'Virtue Ethics Renewed: Morality in a post religious, post relativist secular age', *ResPublica* (2015), accessed online.

17   Pontifical Council for Justice and Peace, *Compendium of the Social Doctrine of the Church* (Rome, 2004), 76.

18   Pope John Paul II, 'Message for the 1999 World Day of Peace', *Acta Apostolicae Sedis 91* (1999), 379.

19   Pope Francis ordered a change to number 2267 of the Catechism of the Catholic Church to reflect this, and gave this teaching a magisterial form in the encyclical *Fratelli tutti* (263), 'Encyclical Letter Fratelli Tutti of the Holy Father Francis on Fraternity and Social Friendship', *The Holy See*.

20   Such as S. Coleridge, R. H. Tawney, W. Temple, J. N. Figgis, and R. Williams. See A. Rowlands, 'Fraternal Traditions: Anglican Social Theology and Catholic Social Teaching in a British Context' in M. Brown ed, *Anglican Social Theology* (London, 2014), 134.

21  S. Spencer, 'R. H. Tawney and Anglican Social Theology', *Crucible: The Journal of Christian Social Ethics* (Jan. 2018), 20.

22  Tawney strongly advocated social equality, aiming to 'narrow the space between valley and peak'. Taxation and greater public expenditure – in particular in the areas of education and health – would allow all people to be treated equally on the grounds of their common humanity. In other words, this was primarily a question of justice.

23  W. Temple, *Christ in his Church* (London, 1925) 81–2.

24  M. J. Sandel, *Justice: What's the Right Thing to Do?* (London, 2010) 143.

25  Sandel claims Rawls offers 'a hollow view of the world, one that refuses to take up discussions of the best way to live'.

26  M. J. Sandel, *Liberalism and the Limits of Justice* (Cambridge, 2010), quoted in N. Sagovsky, *Christian Tradition and the Practice of Justice* (London, 2008), 140. My predecessor and friend Nick Sagovsky has published a brilliant critique of Rawls and Sandel to which I am indebted.

27  N. Sagovsky, *Christian Tradition and the Practice of Justice*, 141.

28 M. J. Sandel, *Liberalism and the Limits of Justice*, 260.

29 *Ibid.*

30 A. Grinnell, 'Forum: Poverty Truth in Leeds', *Crucible: The Journal of Christian Social Ethics* (July 2018).

31 'Humanifesto', *Leeds Poverty Truth Commission*, 2016–2018.

32 'Fratelli tutti', *op. cit.*, 180.

33 'Fratelli tutti', *op. cit.*, 182.

34 'Wellbeing Budget: The Wellbeing Budget 2019', *Te Tai Ōhanga/The Treasury*.

35 P. Selby, *An Idol Unmasked: A Faith Perspective on Money* (London, 2014), 95. See also P. Selby, *Grace and Mortgage: The Language of Faith and the Debt of the World* (London, 1997).

36 B. Latour, *Down to Earth: Politics in the New Climatic Regime* (Cambridge, 2018), 3.

37 *Ibid.*, 38.

38 *Ibid.*, 66.

39 'Encyclical Letter Laudato Si' of the Holy Father Francis on Care for our Common Home', *The Holy See*.

40 'Finland', *Housing First*, accessed online.

41   See H. Quilter-Pinner, 'Finland has found the answer to homelessness. It couldn't be simpler', *The Guardian* (12 May 2018).

42   N. Pleace, D. Culhane, R. Grangelt, and M. Knutagård, 'The Finnish Homelessness Strategy: An International Review', *Reports of the Ministry of the Environment* (Helsinki, 2015).

43   H. Quilter-Pinner, *op. cit.*

44   See Restorative Justice Council website.

45   Professor Jianhong Liu of the University of Macau has outlined some ancient Chinese features of restorative justice, rooted in the teaching of Confucius. Fascinatingly, much of this depends on getting right to the truth of the matter in hand. See J. Liu, 'The Roots of Restorative Justice: Universal Process or from the West to the East?', *Acta Criminologiae et Medicinae Legalis Japonica*, 81 (2015), 1–14.

46   D. Tutu, *No Future Without Forgiveness* (New York, 1999), 22.

47   *Ibid.*, 8.

48   *Ibid.*, 260.

49   H. Matar's *A Month in Siena* (London, 2019) records some beautiful, elegiac reflections on this fresco cycle and its circularity.

50  C. Frugoni, 'The Book of Wisdom and Lorenzetti's Fresco in the Palazzo Pubblico at Siena', *Journal of the Warburg and Courtauld Institutes*, 43 (1980), 43, 239–41.

51  H. Matar, *op. cit.*, 15.

52  P. Marshall, 'Forty Years On: Britain in the EU', *The Round Table* 102/1 (2013).

53  'Fratelli tutti', *op. cit.*, 101.

54  'Laudato si'', *op. cit.*, 240.

55  See John Hughes's exposition of *Deus Caritas est* as 'integralist' thinking in 'Integralism and Gift Exchange in the Anglican Social Tradition', in M. Bullimore ed, *Graced Life: The Writings of John Hughes* (London, 2016), 158.

56  C. Taylor, *A Secular Age* (Cambridge, 2007), 743.

57  C. Dickens, *Bleak House* (London, 1985 [1853]), 33.

58  *Ibid.*

59  K.-C. Tan, 'Does Global Justice Require More Than Just Global Institutions?' *De Ethica: A Journal of Philosophical, Theological and Applied Ethics* 3/1 (2016).

60  See B. Hale, 'Envisioning Justice: the Painter and the Judge' in C. Foster-Gilbert ed, *Art, Imagination and Public Service* (London, 2021).

61  'Whoever destroys a soul amongst Israel (the Jewish people), it is considered as if they destroyed an entire

world. And whoever saves a life amongst Israel, it is considered as if they saved an entire world.' Babylonian Talmud Sanhedrin 37a.

62  J. Senior, *Broken and Betrayed: The True Story of the Rotherham Abuse Scandal by the Woman who Fought to Expose It* (London, 2016).

63  L. Casey, 'Inspection into the governance of Rotherham Council and subsequent intervention', *gov.uk*, 2019, accessed online.

64  Further factors identified include:

- The fear among the town's leaders of causing race-related friction in a town with clearly differentiated ethnic communities. RMBC and the police thought they were acting for the common good by downplaying the ethnicity of those whom the 'sluts' and 'trash' were naming as perpetrators.
- A lack of perspective and knowledge that went largely unchallenged for many years. RMBC officials and police officers did not understand that their decisions and behaviour were utterly at odds with legal requirements especially, but not solely, in respect of those under the age of eighteen.
- Defensiveness about the town's reputation meant that outside scrutiny was not

generally welcome, and the results of
independent reports were dismissed or
simply ignored on the assumption that local
leaders knew best.

- A lack of humility and a failure to recognise
the need to learn meant that training
and resources that could have been made
available were simply not identified or put
into place.

65 Take young people in poverty in the UK: in 2018,
the Joseph Rowntree Foundation estimated that
4.1 million children were living in poverty – a rise
of almost half a million since 2013. That figure
represents 30 per cent of all children resident
in the UK. Definitions of poverty are myriad,
and what might be deemed poverty in the UK
might look like untold riches compared with
living standards in war-torn Yemen or the refugee
camps of Bangladesh. But the general point is
clear: significant numbers of young people in the
UK have significantly reduced opportunities to
thrive compared with the children of wealthier
families. You might also consider young people
and mental health: access to mental health services
for eleven- to eighteen-year-olds is nowhere near
adequate according to a survey (undertaken

by MedeConnect Healthcare) of 1,000 GPs in November 2018. Of the GPs polled, 99 per cent said they feared that eleven- to eighteen-year-olds would come to harm as a direct result of facing long delays to see a specialist and vital care being rationed. According to 90 per cent of GPs, health and social care services for young people who have anxiety, depression, eating disorders, and other conditions were either 'extremely inadequate' (37 per cent) or 'very inadequate' (53 per cent), and only 10 per cent said these services were 'adequate' or 'good'. Many family doctors who took part in the survey said that, in their experience, NHS Child and Adolescent Mental Health Services often could not respond to a sharp increase in demand for care. Experts believe that social media, exam stress, poverty, and challenging family circumstances lie behind the rise.

66 'Universal Declaration of Human Rights', *op. cit.*

67 Thanks to the courage and persistence of a few local residents, the result of the local election in Tower Hamlets held on 22 May 2014 was successfully challenged. Lutfur Rahman was found guilty of electoral fraud and had to stand down as mayor.

68  T. Hobbes, *Leviathan* (1651), pt.1, ch.13, accessed online.

69  W. Brueggemann, 'Justice: The Earthly Form of God's Holiness' in *The Covenanted Self: Explorations in Law and Covenant* (Minneapolis, 1999).

70  The earliest use of the term *tikkun olam*, of which this saying is a translation, is found in the phrase *mip'nei tikkun ha-olam*, 'for the sake of repairing the world', which appears in Mishnah Gittin 4:2.

## WESTMINSTER ABBEY INSTITUTE

*Justice in Public Life* is published in partnership with Westminster Abbey Institute. The Institute was founded by Westminster Abbey in 2013 to work with the people and institutions by whom it is surrounded in Parliament Square, to revitalise moral and spiritual values and virtues in public life. It offers space and time for challenging lectures, conversations, ideas and quiet reflection.

In doing so, the Institute aims to remind those who govern of their vocation to public service, helping them to grow in moral sensitivity and resilience and to better define the good they are trying to do.

The material in this book does not necessarily represent the views of Westminster Abbey or its Institute.

## HAUS CURIOSITIES

### *PUBLISHED WITH WESTMINSTER ABBEY INSTITUTE*

## HAUS CURIOSITIES

Inspired by the topical pamphlets of the interwar years, as well as by Einstein's advice to 'never lose a holy curiosity', the series presents short works of opinion and analysis by notable figures. Under the guidance of the series editor, Peter Hennessy, Haus Curiosities have been published since 2014.

Welcoming contributions from a diverse pool of authors, the series aims to reinstate the concise and incisive booklet as a powerful strand of politico-literary life, amplifying the voices of those who have something urgent to say about a topical theme.

*Commons and Lords: A Short Anthropology of Parliament*
EMMA CREWE

*The European Identity: Historical and Cultural Realities We Cannot Deny*
STEPHEN GREEN

*Breaking Point: The UK Referendum on the EU and its Aftermath*
GARY GIBBON

*Brexit and the British: Who Are We Now?*
STEPHEN GREEN

*These Islands: A Letter to Britain*
ALI M. ANSARI

*Lion and Lamb: A Portrait of British Moral Duality*
MIHIR BOSE

*Drawing the Line: The Irish Border in British Politics*
IVAN GIBBONS

*Not for Patching: A Strategic Welfare Review*
FRANK FIELD AND ANDREW FORSEY

*A Love Affair with Europe: The Case for a European Future*
GILES RADICE

*Fiction, Fact and Future: The Essence of EU Democracy*
JAMES ELLES

*We Are the People: The Rise of the AfD in Germany*
PENNY BOCHUM